A Mom's Guide to Creating

a Magical Life

8 Practical Steps to Feel Happier, Inspired, and More Relaxed

by Kasey Mathews

GREEN WRITERS PRESS   *Brattleboro, Vermont*

Green Writers Press is a Vermont-based publisher whose mission is to spread a message of hope and renewal through the words and images we publish. Throughout we will adhere to our commitment to preserving and protecting the natural resources of the earth. To that end, a percentage of our proceeds will be donated to environmental activist groups and Every Mother Counts—www.everymothercounts.org. Green Writers Press gratefully acknowledges support from individual donors, friends, and readers to help support the environment and our publishing initiative.

Giving Voice to Writers & Artists Who Will Make the World a Better Place
Green Writers Press | Brattleboro, Vermont
www.greenwriterspress.com

ISBN: 978-1-7320815-7-4

COVER & BOOK DESIGN: SARAH CLAREHART

PRINTED ON PAPER WITH PULP THAT COMES FROM FSC-CERTIFIED FORESTS, MANAGED FORESTS THAT GUARANTEE RESPONSIBLE ENVIRONMENTAL, SOCIAL, AND ECONOMIC PRACTICES BY MCNAUGHTON & GUNN, A WOMAN-OWNED BUSINESS CERTIFIED BY THE WOMEN'S BUSINESS ENTERPRISE NATIONAL COUNCIL.

Dedication

 *To my mom, who first showed me the world is a magical place ... to my kids, Andie and Tucker, who fill my days with so much magic ... and to all moms. May you find moments of magic throughout your days.*

WELCOME!

It's truly an honor and a delight to share in this journey of awakening to the magic in your life!

Living a magical life is the richest form of living. It requires believing in your dreams, trusting the Universe as your copilot, setting intentions, taking inspired action, and opening to receive the miracles and magic destined your way. And when you do—look out. Your life will open up in ways you couldn't have imagined possible.

In this guide, you'll learn easy, practical tips to create an extraordinary and magical life—and soon enough, as incredible things begin to happen, you'll hear yourself saying, *"Oh, yeah, you know—it's just the Usual Magic."*

LET'S BEGIN WITH A QUESTION...

Have there been times, over the course of your life, when everything just seemed to line up and unfold perfectly—magically? And have there also been times when it felt as if nothing was going right—as if your world was falling apart?

Recently, this was the case in our family when my son, daughter, husband, and I all experienced significant injuries that required orthopedic surgery. Everyone, from close friends to complete strangers, spoke as if a curse and a dark cloud had enveloped our family.

There were uncertain, gloomy days when I thought they might be right—that maybe we were cursed. Inevitably, though, I'd step back and look with clearer eyes, allowing myself to see all the incredible gifts that had emerged as a result of what we'd been through. I came to see, know, and understand that in the midst of times of ease or difficulty, there is so much opportunity to allow in the magic that is available to us all.

As I came to the realization that magical living is available to each and every one of us, I began to understand how, when, and why magic appears, and to examine the tools we can use to access it all the time. I put on my lab coat and started analyzing the exact elements required to create a life full of meaning, joy, purpose, curiosity, and happiness—in other words, a *Magical Life*.

I hope you'll be as surprised and excited as I was to learn that this way of living is actually quite effortless. All that is required is to let go of old habits and create new ones. It's truly that simple. Imagine yourself removing your glasses with the worn, scratched-up lenses and putting on a new pair with lenses so clear, you see the world in a way you never have before!

Magic has been waiting for you. And if you're here, you know it's time to welcome her into your life. It's time to receive all that you've ever dreamed, hoped, and wished for.

With blessings and love,

Kasey

HOW TO USE THIS GUIDE:

First and foremost, there is no right or wrong way to use this book. However, the more you approach it from a heart-centered place, the greater the potential impact of this work in your life.

Take it at your own pace. Maybe you'll dive right in and work through the book in one sitting, or maybe you'll complete one step a day, or perhaps one a week. This is a gift to you, so choose and do what feels right to you.

You can take it with you to work on when you're sitting in the carpool lane, or when you find a few quiet minutes at work. You could put it on your bedside table and spend time on it in the morning, upon waking, or at night, before going to sleep.

I have provided places for you to write throughout the guidebook, but you may want to use a special notebook/journal to record some of the written exercises. When you find an exercise that really resonates with you, don't hesitate to use it over and over again.

Each step includes a mantra. The intent is for you to use each mantra in a daily meditation. If you just felt yourself contract at the mention of the word *meditation*, don't panic! By *meditation*, I simply mean sitting in a comfortable chair with both feet on the floor and saying the phrase in your head. Eight minutes is ideal for me, so I set the timer on my phone, stream a piece of classical music, and repeat the mantra—that's it. Find what works for you, and give it a try. I'm always astounded at the clarity that comes from such a simple, easy practice.

Most importantly, have fun!

"YOUR HEART IS WHERE THE MAGIC IS, WHERE THE DIVINE IS, WHERE YOUR SOUL SPEAKS...."

Bill Bauman

One
WELCOME YOUR MAGIC

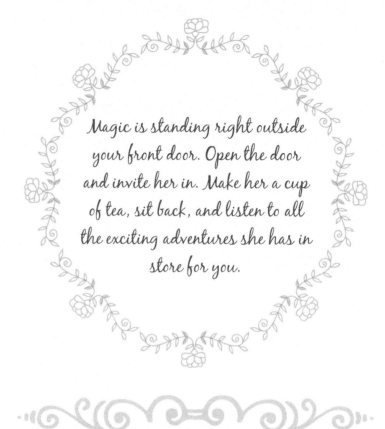

Magic is standing right outside your front door. Open the door and invite her in. Make her a cup of tea, sit back, and listen to all the exciting adventures she has in store for you.

How do you welcome *Magic* into your life? By simply opening yourself up, knowing she's there, and being ready to receive. When you know *Magic* is at work, always thank her for everything she does for you. *Magic* is there when you suddenly think of an old friend who ends up calling you the next day. She's there when you're seeking an answer, and a book falls off the shelf at your feet. And she's there when you feel scared and uncertain and alone, guiding you to know that all will be well. *Magic* is your friend, partner, and guide, and she's always available, ready to help you in any way she can. All you have to do is ask.

> ## "THOSE WHO DON'T BELIEVE IN MAGIC WILL NEVER FIND IT."
>
> *Roald Dahl*

MAGIC HAPPENS:

My daughter's premature birth was one of the scariest, darkest times of my life, yet when I look back, I see there were clearly moments of incredible magic. One, in particular, always stands out. Andie was still living in the hospital an hour away from our home. A huge snowstorm had blanketed Boston, and a cop was waving people away from the closed hospital parking garage. Rolling down my window, I called out and asked where to park, but he shrugged his shoulders and waved for me to keep moving. And then suddenly, in spite of the traffic and honking horns, he walked right over to my car and asked, "How long ya gonna be?" I told him I just wanted a few minutes to see my baby, and without another word, he directed me to a plowed-out space in front of the garage. After spending precious time with Andie, I ran back out and thanked the officer profusely. Just as I was getting back into my car, he called out, "Hey, what's your baby's name?"

"Andie," I called back. "What's yours?"

A big smile lit up his face as he replied, "Andy."

UNLOCK YOUR MAGIC:

Accept Magic's "Friend" Request

* Know that *Magic* is available to you and everyone else.

* *Magic* is guiding you all the time—listen and trust.

* Believe you're worthy of receiving *Magic* in your life.

* If you think, "Hmm, I should call that old friend," then do. Your friend will probably say, "I can't believe you're calling. I was just thinking of you!"

* If you feel like you're supposed to go into a store/café/farm stand, go—and when you find that perfect item on sale or bump into your son's soccer coach who you needed to talk to, you'll know *Magic* is at work.

* Be awake and present enough to see *Magic* as it happens.

* Remember, *Magic* doesn't always appear in the way we expected—there is much magic in times of adversity.

* Always offer *Magic* your thanks.

* Ask for what you want and need.

* Don't "push" or try to force *Magic*—trust and know that the timing is perfect, and if it is in your highest and best interest, *Magic* will arrive in perfect timing.

* Look for signs—guideposts to lead you in the right direction.

MAKE YOUR MAGIC:

Create two to-do lists—one for *you* and one for *Magic!* Fold a blank piece of paper in half. On one side, write "My To-Do List," and on the other, "*Magic's* To-Do List." Fill out your to-do list with anything you need to get done today.

Then fill out *Magic's* list. These are things you wish would happen, but you're not sure how—areas in which you could use a little divine guidance!

My To-Do List

answer outstanding emails

bake/pick up cookies for school bake sale

go to yoga class

reschedule doctor's appointment

pick up kids for soccer

Magic's To-Do List

the perfect tutor/mentor arrives in my son's life

the ideal part-time job I've been seeking becomes available

an amazing, affordable vacation is offered to our family

I find a writing group

MAGIC MANTRA:

"I am worthy and ready to receive all the magic the Universe has in store for me."

If I had a magic wand, I would...

_____

_____

_____

_____

_____

_____

_____

Magic wants to make all your wishes and dreams come true. She claps her hands in delight whenever she hears the words "Thank you!"

Two
EXPRESS GRATITUDE

Ah, gratitude.... It's easy to express when we receive what we love—what we desire. *Thank you*—the two magic words we're taught as soon as we can talk. Over time, they become almost automatic. Yet it's when we offer our thanks—and truly feel it—that it really seems to matter. You see, gifts are coming to us all the time: from that amazing parking space to the unexpected job opportunity. It's up to us to notice these moments and express our gratitude. Have you ever given a gift, and the recipient was so genuinely grateful, you couldn't wait to give another? That's how it works with *Magic*. The more gratitude you express, the more magical gifts—both big and small—appear in your life. And sometimes, gifts arrive in unexpected packages, which at first may not seem like gifts at all...yet they reveal themselves in time. So keep your eyes wide open, notice all the gifts coming your way, and always offer your gratitude and thanks in return.

> "WHEN YOU LOOK AT THE WORLD THROUGH THE EYES OF GRATITUDE, THE WORLD BECOMES A MAGICAL AND AMAZING PLACE."
>
> *Jennifer Gayle*

MAGIC HAPPENS:

I was late to pick up the kids at school, but I'd promised my son, Tucker, that I'd buy him the book he needed. The bookstore was on the way, but I really didn't have time. Right in front of the store, the light turned red, and I got a strong sense that I was supposed to go in. As I raced to the register with the book in hand, a sign caught my eye: the author of the book that had been my lifeline while my daughter was in the hospital would be signing books there the very next day!

The next afternoon, I packed up my well-loved copy of the book and headed back to the bookstore. At the end of the reading, I mustered up the courage to tell the author how much her book had comforted me after my daughter's birth. It turned out her brother was sitting next to me, and had had a premature baby just the year before. I told him and the author about the book I'd been working on— *Preemie: Lessons in Love, Life, and Motherhood*—and not only did she mentor me through the publishing process, she wrote the quote on the back of the book! *Magic* was at work once again!

UNLOCK YOUR MAGIC:

Look for the gifts coming your way.

- When gifts arrive, say thank you.

- You can thank whomever/whatever feels right to you—*Magic*, the Universe, God, your spirit guides, angels, your higher self.

- Don't overlook the small gifts. You'd never open a gift and say, "This is all you got me?" Express gratitude for gifts of all sizes.

- What may appear as a negative occurrence in your life could be a gift in disguise. Think of a time when this may have been the case. For example, when my daughter injured her knee placing soccer and was at the hospital having surgery, I was NOT seeing the injury as a gift. Now, I see all the incredible adult mentors who have come into her life, and know that this "unfortunate event" may end up being one of the most formative moments of her life.

- Trust that *Magic* always has your back.

- Have gratitude for things exactly as they are.

- Make gratitude your superpower!

MAKE YOUR MAGIC:

Before bed tonight, write down three things that happened today for which you're grateful. You may be surprised at the wonderful sleep that arrives as a result. Try it with your kids—as you tuck them in, ask them to name three happy things that happened for them today. Before you know it, this may become a nightly routine!

3 things I am grateful for today…

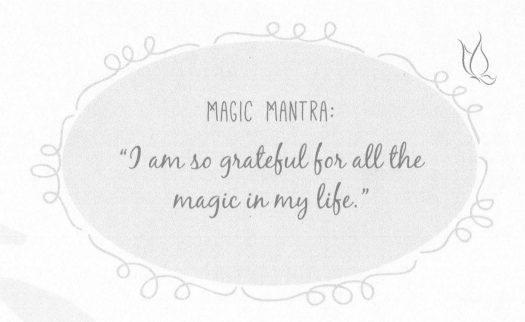

MAGIC MANTRA:

"I am so grateful for all the magic in my life."

When I close my eyes and see the life of my dreams, it looks like...

_____

_____

_____

_____

_____

_____

_____

_____

Take Magic's hand and follow her down that overgrown path. See it opening up before you—leading you straight back into your own heart.

Three
DISCOVER WHAT YOU LOVE

Let's take a little journey back in time–back before you became grown-up you, the you who takes on grown-up responsibilities, the grown-up you who cares for everyone else and puts her own needs last. Let's go back to that time, and get a glimpse of what she loved. Did she love to dance, paint, hike, sleep till noon on Saturdays? Let's find out and bring a bit of her back, because she's the one who calls in *Magic*. She's the one who whispers in your ear, "Come on, let's play!"

> ## "LOVE IS THE CLOSEST THING WE HAVE TO MAGIC."
>
> *Unknown*

MAGIC HAPPENS:

This isn't a pack-your-bag, leave-a-note-on-the-kitchen-counter-and-fly-off-to-Aruba kind of magic. This is more subtle, and involves finding everyday moments of magic in the midst of your busy, messy, responsibility-laden life. This is about remembering what feeds your soul, and taking little bites throughout the day. I love color and art, but life doesn't exactly afford many trips to museums these days. Instead, I look for moments of color and beauty throughout my days. On walks in the woods, I notice the bright green leaves on the trees and the moss on the ground. At the grocery store, I walk slowly through the produce section, taking in the colors of the red strawberries, orange and yellow peppers, and bright green grapes. And on days when I have a bit of spare time, I'll wander through the local shabby-chic antique shop, or stop at the greenhouse for what my Aunt Mimi calls "flower therapy." I let my gaze soften, and wander amongst the flowers and plants, soaking in their magic.

UNLOCK YOUR MAGIC:

Ask yourself: What do I love?

🦢 Discover/uncover/rediscover what brings you joy and feeds your soul.

🦢 Think of something you haven't done in so long that you used to love to do!

🦢 Discover the little things you can do to make your life flow with more ease and grace.

🦢 How would it feel to be centered, nourished, and focused, with the ability to give back to yourself just as you give to everyone else?

🦢 Time is precious—seek and find special moments just for you.

🦢 You decide what makes you happy and fulfilled.

🦢 Remember, "It's OK to love what you love." —Debra Poneman, *Your Year of Miracles*

MAKE YOUR MAGIC:

Sit quietly, with your eyes closed. Take a big breath in, exhale it out, and see yourself walking down a beautiful path. Feel the warm sun on your back. Keep walking until you come to a patch of green grass, where a large quilt is spread out. In the center is a wooden picnic basket. Open the lid and see what's inside. Everything in the basket is just for you! This is a magic basket, so don't worry about size or shape—you can pull all your wishes, wants, and desires out of this basket. When you're ready, slowly open your eyes and write down all the delights you found in the basket. Stay in your heart, and just write. If your head tries to jump in, hold a hand on your heart, take a few deep breaths, and say, "I got this."

MAGIC MANTRA:

"I invite all I love to appear in my life."

...and then Magic said, "Rest, little one," and lit a vanilla candle, pulled the blanket up to your chin, and sang a song so sweet and soft, you felt it in the center of your soul.

Four
GREET MAGIC
with Your
VERY BEST SELF

You take care of everyone else, right? So, who takes care of you? That's what I thought. At some point, if you don't care for yourself as you do everyone else, your well is going to run dry. Let's refill your well so you have plenty to give yourself and everyone else in your life! The three basic elements you need are: rest, proper nutrition, and movement. And if you really want your well to spill over with joyous excess— remember to make time for what you love!

> "BY ACCEPTING YOURSELF AND FULLY BEING WHAT YOU ARE, YOUR SIMPLE PRESENCE CAN MAKE OTHERS HAPPY. YOU YOURSELF, AS MUCH AS ANYBODY IN THE ENTIRE UNIVERSE, DESERVE YOUR LOVE AND AFFECTION."
>
> *Buddha*

MAGIC HAPPENS:

Years ago, my dear friend was diagnosed with acute cancer. She was married to the love of her life and raising three young kids, and everyone was terrified for their future. My friend is a testament to the fact that miracles happen. Eight years later, she's healthier than ever! And every time I see her, she looks incredible—dressed in skirts, boots, and lots of jewelry. One day, I commented, "You always look so amazing." She smiled and said the words I'll forever carry in my heart: "Kase, I looked in my closet and saw all those clothes hanging there waiting for the party. And then I realized—*this is the party*." This is the party. So what are you waiting for?

UNLOCK YOUR MAGIC:

- 🌿 **Rest.** Eight hours a night is ideal. Three nights in a row, go to bed at 10:00 p.m., and see how you feel.

- 🌿 **Nutrition.** Eat foods that come from the earth, fresh and organic whenever possible.
  Start your day with breakfast. My two favorites are avocado on gluten-free toast or hot quinoa with cranberries, pumpkin seeds, and maple syrup. I use a rice maker, so the quinoa is perfectly cooked and ready in the a.m.!

- 🌿 **Drink lots of water.** Find yourself a special glass you love, and refill it all day long.

- 🌿 **Movement.** If you have a gym membership—go! Otherwise, walk outside, put on music and dance, or try a 30-minute online yoga video. Just move your body! I'm motivated by a reward, so each week, I make a chart. If I exercise four times a week for 45 minutes, or five times a week for 30, I buy myself fresh flowers! What reward would motivate you?

- 🌿 Remember—*this* is the party, and *Magic* loves a party!

MAKE YOUR MAGIC:

Even when you know exactly what you need to take care of yourself, does it ever feel like you're not allowed? Like you're being selfish? Well, you're not. Taking care of yourself is a gift to you and your loved ones—so give yourself permission, and take time for what you need.

Fill out the permission slip and give yourself permission to take care of you!

Having trouble deciding? Here are a few suggestions. Nap in the middle of the day, sit outside and read a book, leave work and go for a run, meet a friend for lunch, stay in your PJs and watch an old romantic comedy, or make a tray of cheese, chocolate, and red wine and pretend you're in France. It's up to you—you've been granted permission!

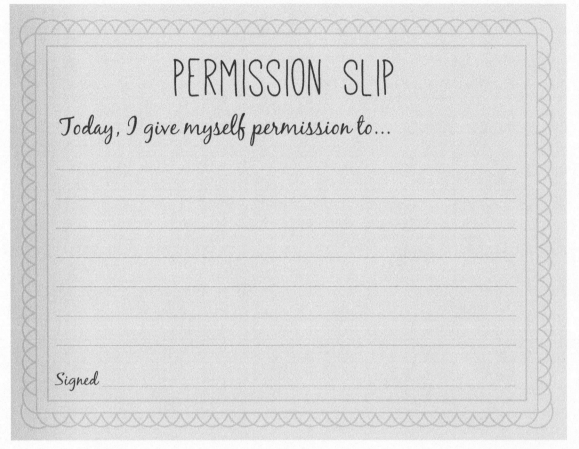

PERMISSION SLIP

Today, I give myself permission to...

_____

_____

_____

_____

_____

_____

Signed _____

MAGIC MANTRA:

"I love and care for me."

I feel loved and cared for when...

_____

_____

_____

_____

_____

_____

...she took the to-do list from your hand and led you to the backyard, where you sat knee to knee making bracelets out of dandelion stems.

Five
WAKE UP
and Become More
PRESENT IN YOUR LIFE

Living a magical life is about waking up—becoming conscious and present in (and to) the life you're living. It's more than just going through the motions of daily life. It's about slowing down and noticing the wonder of a sticky plate of half-eaten pancakes, the touch of freshly-laundered clothes, and the smell of morning coffee. As you practice becoming more present—more awake in your day-to-day life—you also become more attuned to your gut feelings, or intuitive guidance. When you follow that guidance, *Magic* is usually there waiting for you.

> ## "FOREVER IS COMPOSED OF NOWS."
>
> *Emily Dickinson*

MAGIC HAPPENS:

Before the Amish decide what technology to allow into their lives, they try it out to see how it impacts their day-to-day living. When the telephone first became widely available, they learned that folks would ride for miles in their horse-drawn buggies to visit friends, only to find that the host's focus immediately shifted to the person on the phone, diverting attention away from their guests. And with that, phones were no longer a part of their culture. Consider that the next time you're having lunch with a friend, in the car with your kids, or gathered at the dinner table, and your phone rings or you get a text. Try to stay present with those right in front of you.

UNLOCK YOUR MAGIC:

- Be present and centered, and do just one activity at a time—washing dishes, folding laundry, watching your child at the park.

- Become more conscious of how you spend your days.

- Put down the cell phone. If your nose is in a screen and *Magic* is right in front of you, you'll miss her.

- Create an email routine, and limit it to three times a day: morning, noon, and night.

- Become more aware of your gut feelings.

MAKE YOUR MAGIC:

1. **Practice awareness** by looking at things in your day-to-day life as if you're seeing them for the first time.

2. **Focus** on what's right in front of you.

3. **Be conscious of your breathing.** *Are* you breathing? Take a big breath in, and let it back out. Do this throughout your day.

4. **Check in with you.** Ask yourself, "Am I present?" The answer may surprise you!

I look around myself and see...

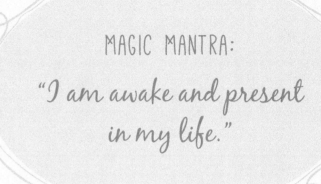

MAGIC MANTRA:

"I am awake and present in my life."

Six
MAKE SPACE FOR MAGIC IN YOUR LIFE

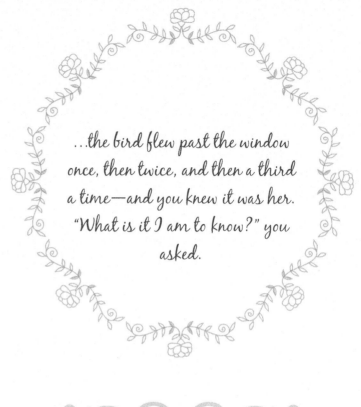

...the bird flew past the window once, then twice, and then a third a time—and you knew it was her. "What is it I am to know?" you asked.

Imagine you have finally found the perfect living-room chair (and it was on sale!). You bring it home, but the room is already full of furniture. Do you just cram it in, or randomly take something out? Of course not. Instead, you step back, see how you can rearrange things, and decide what is worth keeping and what's not. The same holds true for *Magic*. You need to make room for what you're welcoming into your life, both inside and out.

> "AS I UNCLUTTER MY LIFE, I FREE MYSELF TO ANSWER THE CALLINGS OF MY SOUL."
>
> *Unknown*

MAGIC HAPPENS:

Consider this Zen teaching, which identifies the emotional concerns we carry that are unhelpful, if not harmful, to our well-being. Two monks are walking down the road and come across a young woman dressed in fine silks, standing before a stream she clearly cannot cross without ruining her clothes. Without a word, the older of the two picks her up and carries her across the stream, setting her down on the other side. The monks continue walking, and several hours later, the younger monk finally says, "We are not even allowed to make eye contact with a woman, and you picked that woman up." To this, the older monk replies, "My brother, I set her down hours ago—it is you who has been carrying her all this way."

UNLOCK YOUR MAGIC:

- More emotional space = more magic

- Be aware of your home environment. Is there unnecessary noise? Clutter you can get rid of? Everything we own carries an energy with it. Let go of old, unwanted items, and make room for what you really want.

- The Universe is like a vacuum—space that is freed up will be filled with what you're seeking.

- Be selective about who and what you let into your life.

- Learn to create boundaries and say no.

- Before agreeing to anything, check in with yourself, and ask: *Is this something I really want to do?*

- Turn off the news, and keep your energy and vibration high.

- Surround yourself with what you love.

MAKE YOUR MAGIC:

Internal Space-Clearing

Fear loves to hide in the dark recesses of our being, where it can breed and grow. When we write our fears down or speak them out loud, they are brought to the light and lose much of their power.

On a blank sheet of paper, finish the thought "I am worried that _____." And again, "I am worried that _____." And again, "I am worried that _____."

Repeat this until you feel a big breath enter, and then let a big breath out. Sit for a few minutes with this release technique, which creates a new, internal, spacious feeling. Try this when you feel scattered and unable to stay focused. Often, fear is beneath the surface, cluttering your heart and mind.

I am worried that ... _____

I am worried that ... _____

I am worried that ... _____

I am worried that ... _____

I am worried that ... _____

I am worried that ... _____

_____

_____

27

MAKE YOUR MAGIC:

External Space-Clearing

Try this Feng Shui clutter cleanse. Each day, remove 27 items from your home—either give them away or throw them away, for nine days in a row. With just a quick glance around your house, you can probably find a hundred things to let go of, but only do 27 each day. That way, you'll avoid feeling overwhelmed and burned out by day three. By days eight and nine, you may be searching for items to let go of—counting individual magazines or earrings to make up your 27 items! Have fun—and here's how to hold yourself accountable. If you miss a day, the exercise requires you to start back at day one!

MAGIC MANTRA:

"I create space for Magic in my life."

I want to make space for …

...she turned to you, took both your cheeks between her soft hands, looked you in the eye, and said, "It is all yours. All you have to do is ask."

Seven

ACTIVELY CREATE MAGIC

As you've followed the steps in creating your *Magical Life*, perhaps you've begun to notice some changes. Are you feeling more grounded and present in your daily life? Are you happier, and do you have more energy? Now it's time to open yourself up even more, and begin consciously attracting *Magic*. Know for certain that there is an abundant supply of incredible blessings just waiting for you.

> ## "YOU'LL SEE IT WHEN YOU BELIEVE IT."
> *Wayne Dyer*

MAGIC HAPPENS:

Years ago, when our son entered kindergarten, the program in which we enrolled him was a disappointment. At one point, I was so frustrated, I said, "I wish we could just move, and find some alternative school that teaches to the way he learns." Less than two years later, my husband was offered a job further north, and as we stood in a school that was a perfect fit for our son, I suddenly remembered my declaration and realized the Universe had been listening! That was when we decided to try to find a new home that was also a perfect fit. My husband, son, daughter, and I all wrote down in great detail everything we wanted and hoped for in a new house. Sure enough, we found an old fixer-upper farmhouse with apple trees, stones walls, and a big sledding hill that had magically been on the market for two years—just waiting for us!

UNLOCK YOUR MAGIC:

- Look for signs, and allow yourself to be guided toward your desires.

- Have the courage to ask for what you want.

- Write down exactly what you want—the more detail, the better!

- When writing down your intentions, be mindful of the positive and negative aspects of your language. If you're hoping to overcome an illness, don't use the word *illness* in your intention, or you risk attracting more. Instead, phrase your intention as something along the lines of "I am well, and in wonderful health." Notice how that intention statement is written as if it has already come to be. Avoid the use of the word "want," or you'll simply attract more wanting. Notice the difference in these two statements: "We want the house of our dreams" versus "We are living in the house of our dreams."

- Write it down as if it's already a reality, and it will become one!

- Be mindful of your thoughts. Like the language you speak, thoughts are energy, and very powerful.

MAKE YOUR MAGIC:

Sit in a comfortable chair, close your eyes, and take a few deep, centering breaths. Then finish the statement: "What I really want is...." Write down the very first answer that comes to mind.

Once you know the answer, restate it using positive language. Most importantly, keep it in the present tense. For example, "I really want a new job" becomes "I am so happy in my new job."

Declare your intention to the Universe by writing it down on the next page.

What I really want is ...

MAGIC MANTRA:

Write your statement here from "Make Your Magic," and you've just created your own mantra! Say it loud and clear, and remember, the Universe is listening!

My mantra is …

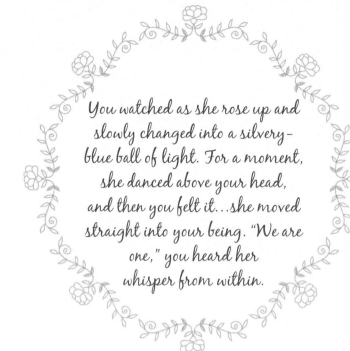

You watched as she rose up and slowly changed into a silvery-blue ball of light. For a moment, she danced above your head, and then you felt it...she moved straight into your being. "We are one," you heard her whisper from within.

Eight
CELEBRATE YOUR MAGIC and Share It with Others!

You are a wondrous, magnificent being, who was put here on Earth to be the unique, amazing person that you are. Allow your gifts, light, and radiance to shine through. Share it with others, so they, too, can become all they are meant to be. As you continue to move through life, ever expanding, opening, and allowing in all the *Magic* in store for you, know that you are so blessed, so loved, and so adored. And know that *Magic* is a part of you—it's time to celebrate and play!

> "JOY IS WHAT HAPPENS TO US WHEN WE ALLOW OURSELVES TO RECOGNIZE HOW GOOD THINGS REALLY ARE."
>
> *Marianne Williamson*

MAGIC HAPPENS:

A few weeks after my first book, *Preemie: Lessons in Love, Life, and Motherhood* was released, I was traveling to speak at an event in front of a large crowd in Fort Worth, Texas. The airport parking garage was full, which meant a satellite lot and a shuttle bus to the airport. I was already nervous about my talk, so this just made me more stressed. On the bus, the only seat left was next to an older gentleman. The gentleman, whose name I later learned was Jim, asked me where I was headed. We chatted about my book, and then about his daughters. Just as we were about to get off the bus, a little voice in my head suggested I give him a copy of my book. I was reluctant, because all my other copies had been shipped to the event, and it was the only copy I had with me—but I honored the voice, and put the book in his hand. Six months later, I received a letter. "I'm not sure if you'll remember me, but a while back, we rode a bus together, and you gave me a copy of your book." I smiled, remembering Jim. Then I read on: "Your beautiful story and positive outcome were, for me, the encouragement and validation I needed to help my wife and me through the deep grief of losing our daughter in January."

I keep that letter in the top drawer of my desk, and often think of the circumstances that had to occur that day in order for our paths to cross. I'm comforted in the knowledge that even if we don't realize it in the moment, we are always being guided.

UNLOCK YOUR MAGIC:

🌿 Magic loves to play! Have fun with her—take her for walks in the woods, go on the swings at the park, or dance in the middle of the day!

🌿 Could it be that igniting your magic and sharing it with others is one of your purposes in life?

🌿 Take care of you in the best possible way you know how. Open yourself up to all the magical wonders of your world, and show up in the world to spread your magic and love.

🌿 Be spontaneous! Surprise yourself and *Magic* by doing something out of the ordinary: write a letter to an old friend, do a cartwheel on the lawn, or go to the movies by yourself on a Tuesday night!

🌿 Recognize that all the answers and *Magic* are inside you—they have been all along. You are the magic, and the magic is within you!

🌿 It is your birthright to receive all the goodness and love you are being offered.

🌿 Open your heart, hands, and mind, and allow your *Magical Life* to unfold! Let the ripples spread out from you and touch everyone else in your life.

MAKE YOUR MAGIC:

Today, practice offering your complete and full attention to three different people in your life. Notice how they respond when they know they have your full, undivided attention. And notice if you see a change in how they seem to feel about themselves. Try it with your kids, a colleague, your partner; give it a go with the cashier at the store. Notice their name tag. When they ask how your day is going, look them in the eye when you respond, and offer a genuine response beyond the standard "Fine, thanks." Notice the smiles and little sparks of magic that ignite as a result. As French philosopher Simone Weil said, "Attention is the rarest and purest form of generosity."

MAGIC MANTRA:

I am deeply loved, and meant to share my magic with the world.

I hope you have found this guidebook helpful and inspiring, and that you're finding more *Magic* in your life!

A Gift

A companion to this guide, ***The Magical Living Daily Planner***, is a way to organize your days in a more soulful way. This fun and simple approach will leave you feeling more grounded, productive, and joyful every day!

An Invitation

If you'd like to take a deeper dive into this work, I offer you an invitation—a complimentary **30-minute Magical Living Discovery Session**. Together, we will uncover all the blocks and limiting beliefs that are holding you back from living your *Magical Life!*

To receive your gift, discovery session, or both, please visit **www.kaseymathews.com**.

With blessings and love,

Kasey

> "Loving myself is my magic wand."
>
> Louise Hay

Acknowledgements

Deepest gratitude to my amazing designer, Sarah Clarehart. Sarah, you have the incredible ability to understand what I see in my head and bring it to life on the page and computer screen. You continually astound me, and I feel so blessed to have you in my life.

Dede Cummings, you've gone from being my agent to my publisher, and continue to be one of the most inspiring and dynamic women I've ever met. I'm so grateful to you, Cathryn Lykes, and the wonderful team at Green Writers Press. It's an honor and privilege to be part of a publishing house whose mission is "to spread a message of hope and renewal through words and images...and adhere to our commitment to preserving and protecting the natural resources of the earth."

Finally, to my husband, Lee, and children, Tucker and Andie. You three have made my life more magical than I ever imagined possible.